Breaking the Bondage to Fear

BREAKING THE BONDAGE TO FEAR:
Teachings from the Book of Romans

By Ekron Malcolm

Ekron Malcolm

Breaking The Bondage to Fear:
Teachings from The Book of Romans

Copyright © 2023 Reverend Ekron Malcolm

Unless otherwise specified, all scripture quotations are taken from the Authorized King James Version.

Scripture quotations marked NIV are from the New International Version of the Bible Copyright © 1973, 1978, and 1984 by the International Bible Society.
Zondervan Bible Publishers, Grand Rapids, Michigan

All rights reserved. No part of this publication may be reproduced, stored in a retrieval system, or transmitted in any form or by any means without prior permission of the copyright owner.

Table of Contents

Introduction 7

Chapter 1 10

The Effects of Fear 10

    Understanding Fear 10

Chapter 2 18

Romans' Road to Courage 18

    The Role of Faith 19

    Central Elements in Overcoming Fear 21

Chapter 3 26

The Spirit of Adoption 26

    Fear vs. Adoption 26

    The Sense of Belonging & Security 30

    Prayer of Thankfulness 36

Chapter 4 39

Walking in Victory 39

    Embracing The Power of Faith 40

    Resilience in the Face of Setbacks 41

Ekron Malcolm

- Renewing the Mind 42
- Biblical Examples of Victory 44
- Prayers of Faith and Commitment 50

Chapter 5 .... *53*

Embracing God's Love to Conquer Fear *53*

- Choosing God's Love Over Fear 54
- Prayer to Cultivate God's Love 58

Chapter 6 .... *60*

The Art of Christian Meditation *60*

- Dwelling on God's Word 60
- The Essence of Christian Meditation 65
- The Role of Daily Meditation 65
- Musing on God's Word 65
- The Transformative Power of Meditation 66
- A Source of Renewed Mindsets 66
- Daily Meditation for Fearless Living 67
- Scriptures for Daily Meditation 68
- Prayer to Cultivate God's Power 70

Chapter 7 .... *72*

Encouragement for the Journey *72*

Breaking the Bondage to Fear

> Key Takeaways 72
> Discussion Questions for Further Reflection 75
> Prayers for Breaking Patterns of Habitual Sins 77
> APPENDICES 80
> More Helpful Resources 80
> Holy Spirit Counselling Corner 81
> Spiritual Counselling Questions 83
> About the Author 88

Ekron Malcolm

Acknowledgments

I offer my deepest gratitude to The Lord Jesus Christ, the ultimate source of wisdom and inspiration. Your presence has guided me on every word and illuminated the path to breaking the bondage to fear with faith.

Ekron Malcolm
Toronto, Ontario
November 2023

Breaking the Bondage to Fear

Introduction

If you are struggling with fears that seem unnatural, then help is on the way. First, let me encourage you through the pages of these teachings from Romans, which lays a foundation for all who are struggling to break free from the agitating, oppressive forces and fears that try to keep them bound and unproductive in life. You will find other resources at the back of this book to help you break free from bondage and to find freedom in Christ Jesus.

In a world defined by unpredictability and trials, fear often emerges as an unwelcome companion on our life's journey, manifesting in various forms that hinder our growth and happiness. "Breaking The Bondage to Fear: Teachings from the Book of Romans" offers a profound exploration of fear's intricate layers, drawing inspiration from the timeless wisdom of the Book of Romans. This compelling book takes you on a transformative journey, dissecting the essence of fear and guiding you toward a life illuminated by courage and unwavering faith.

The Book of Romans provides a blueprint for courage, with faith as its guiding star. Through the wisdom of Romans, we uncover the keys to unlocking our inner reservoirs of strength, empowering us to confront and overcome our deepest fears. We embark on a transformative path toward freedom, casting off the shackles of fear and embracing life unrestrained.

Ekron Malcolm

Conquering fear is not just a distant possibility but an attainable reality. We embark on a journey to develop a mindset that steadfastly rejects fear, and instead, explores the might of faith, the cultivation of resilience in the face of setbacks, and the art of reshaping thought patterns that once imprisoned us. At the heart of our exploration lies the ultimate remedy for fear: profound and unwavering love. By deeply understanding God's love, we unearth the strength and courage to cast fear aside, enabling us to lead a life filled with purpose, confidence, and fulfillment.

"Breaking The Bondage to Fear: Teachings from the Book of Romans" guides you in conquering fear, while offering a path to embrace a life illuminated by courage, faith, and love. The hidden treasures within the Book of Romans empower you to transcend fear and claim the life you are destined to live.

The teachings in this book encourage those seeking freedom in Christ from slavery to fear and other struggles to confront fear, unmask its various forms, and ultimately discover the path to becoming conquerors in Christ.

The central theme of Breaking the Bondage to Fear revolves around the reality that true liberation from fear requires a holistic approach. It is not enough to tackle fear solely at the surface level; instead, we must simultaneously fortify the mind, emotions, and spiritual foundation. The book guides you through practical strategies to strengthen your mental resilience, emotional well-being, and spiritual positioning, creating a comprehensive toolkit for breaking free from fear's suffocating grip.

Breaking the Bondage to Fear

Chapter 1

The Effects of Fear

Romans 8:15, "For ye have not received the spirit of bondage again to fear, but ye have received the Spirit of adoption, whereby we cry, Abba, Father."

Fear. It's a word that carries immense power and significance in our lives. It's an emotion we all experience at one point or another, an innate response hardwired into our very beings. The caution of fear can be a friend, warning us of danger and keeping us safe. Still, fear itself can also be a formidable foe, paralyzing and holding us back from reaching our full potential.

Understanding Fear

Fear is a complex and multi-faceted emotion, and it's important to distinguish between healthy fear, which serves as a protective mechanism, and irrational or debilitating fear, which hinders our progress. Healthy fear alerts us to danger, such as a looming physical threat, prompting what is commonly known as "fight-or-flight" response. This fear is a natural and essential part of our

Breaking the Bondage to Fear

survival toolkit. On the other hand, irrational fear, which brings about irrational feelings and is often rooted in anxiety or past traumas, can be paralyzing. It can manifest as phobias, panic attacks, or a constant sense of unease that prevents us from living our lives to the fullest. This form of fear most often holds us back from realizing our dreams.

The physical manifestations of fear hold a remarkable power over our bodies, and their impact can be profoundly challenging. When fear takes root, it triggers a cascade of physiological responses. Our bodies instinctively prepare for a perceived threat, activating the fight-or-flight response. As our heart rate quickens, our muscles tense, and our breathing becomes shallow, these immediate changes prepare us for rapid action. While this reaction is crucial in genuine life-threatening situations, it becomes problematic when fear is chronic or irrational. Prolonged stress responses due to anxiety can have severe consequences, affecting various bodily systems.

The long-term effects of fear on the body are well-documented, as stated in the Chronic Stress News Research Article. Chronic stress and anxiety can lead to an increased risk of heart disease, hypertension, and weakened immune function. The continuous secretion of stress hormones, such as cortisol, may disrupt sleep patterns and lead to insomnia, fatigue, and impaired cognitive functioning. Furthermore, individuals who find themselves trapped in a state of enduring fear are at an elevated risk of developing issues, including but not limited to anxiety, depression, and post-traumatic stress disorder. Therefore, it is crucial to recognize the physical toll that fear can exact on our bodies, underscoring the importance of addressing and conquering fear with faith and resilience for our overall well-being.

The physical effects of fear can also manifest in our daily lives, affecting our health and well-being. Romans 12:11 encourages us to be "not slothful in business; fervent in spirit; serving the Lord." Fear can lead to a sense of slothfulness, sapping our physical energy and motivation. This passage reminds us to be fervent in spirit and to serve the Lord enthusiastically, offering a path to counteract the physical effects of fear by focusing on our spiritual connection and purpose. In doing so, we can regain our physical vitality and strength, even facing challenges posed by fear.

Fear often arises from the pressures and expectations of the world, pushing us to conform and adopt a mindset of anxiety and insecurity. However, through faith, prayer, and a renewed mind, we can break free from these chains, discovering God's "good, acceptable, and perfect will." In this transformation, we can find healing for the emotional, physical, and spiritual wounds inflicted by fear, knowing that His perfect love casts out all fear.

Fear is not a recent development in the human experience; it's deeply ingrained in our history. Early humans who were vigilant and cautious had a higher chance of survival. Fear, in this sense, was a survival advantage. Today, we may not face the same life-threatening dangers as others in the past, but our brains and bodies still respond similarly to perceived threats. Racing hearts, sweaty palms, and heightened alertness are natural responses to danger.

Fear isn't limited to life-threatening situations. It manifests in countless forms in our modern world. The fear of failure prevents

Breaking the Bondage to Fear

us from pursuing our dreams, the fear of rejection keeps us from forming deep and meaningful relationships, and the fear of the unknown keeps us from exploring new horizons. We encounter many fears daily in today's fast-paced and often chaotic world. Fear of missing out (FOMO) can lead to anxiety about not keeping up with others on social media. Fear of judgment can cause us to silence our authentic selves. Fear of economic instability can keep us in unfulfilling jobs. The list goes on.

Fear, both spiritual and emotional, can leave a profound impact on our lives, affecting our well-being in many ways. In Romans 8:15, it is written, "For ye have not received the spirit of bondage again to fear, but ye have received the Spirit of adoption, whereby we cry, Abba, Father." This verse highlights fear's spiritual and emotional effects – it can enslave our minds, making us feel trapped and distant from God's loving embrace. The emotional weight of fear and anxiety can be paralyzing, leading to feelings of isolation, insecurity, and despair.

Take note of the Apostle Paul's teachings on fear: he describes it as a spirit of bondage. Within Satan's arsenal lies the spirit of fear. This force ensnares and enslaves, subjecting individuals to its influence of negative emotions and feelings. As believers, we are not recipients of such a spirit; we have received the Spirit of adoption; that is the reason we can triumph over the onslaught of the spirit of fear, as it does not rightfully belong to us and merely seeks to imprison us in the bondage of sin. Anything originating from the realm of darkness is inherently deceptive and should neither be trusted nor accepted.

To understand this better, let's look at the passage in Romans 8:5-6 which says, "For to be carnally minded is death, but to be spiritually minded is life and peace." The spirit of fear, which comes from the realm of darkness, endeavours to impact our lives by instilling debilitating negative emotions. This spirit can oppress us when we deviate from living according to the spiritual nature of Christ within. When our desires and actions align with the desires of the flesh and are driven by carnal thinking, we inadvertently open ourselves to the spiritual forces of darkness. This misalignment creates a vulnerability, making it easier for the forces of darkness to operate in our lives. These forces may manifest as oppression, fear, doubt, and a pervasive sense of unease, casting a shadow over our spiritual and emotional well-being.

In this context, it becomes crucial to recognize the profound interplay between our spiritual and mental states. When we are attuned to the spiritual nature of Christ within us, we experience a deep sense of alignment and divine guidance. However, when the carnal mind dominates our desires and thought patterns, we open ourselves to negative spiritual influences that can obscure our path, breeding fear and uncertainty. Understanding these dynamics underscores the importance of seeking spiritual alignment and nurturing our faith in Christ to resist the spirit of fear and regain the peace and assurance that only spiritual unity can bring.

To be delivered from bondage to fear, believers must live "according to the Spirit." A believer's mindset and actions must align with the guidance of the Word of God and the empowerment of the Holy Spirit. This transformation is a process as the believer, empowered by the Holy Spirit, gradually overcomes the captivating patterns of sin and disobedience. By choosing to live

Breaking the Bondage to Fear

according to the principles of the Spirit, believers can break free from the entanglements of bondage, embrace a life of liberty and righteousness, and experience the peace that comes from a restored relationship with God.

Fear has profound physical and emotional effects, often enveloping us in a grip that can be challenging to break free from; however, we have the promise of "life and peace." This promise is for everyone who believes, and to walk in this promise, we need to believe that it is ours and that we have the right to have it because Jesus, our Lord and Saviour, has paid the ultimate price through His death and resurrection to secure it for us.

The phrase "ultimate price" underlines the magnitude of Jesus' sacrifice, emphasizing the gravity of His actions to secure our well-being. His death on the cross and triumphant resurrection paved the way for us to inherit the promised life and peace. Through this act, Jesus dismantled the barriers that could hinder us from fully embracing the abundant life and peace God intends for His believers.

Believing in this promise is an active, intentional choice. It involves aligning our thoughts, attitudes, and actions with the truth that we are beneficiaries of God's gracious promise. By doing so, we navigate life with purpose, security, and peace, drawing from the wellspring of assurance and hope in Christ's redemptive work. We have been given not only a promise but an invitation to live a life grounded in the unwavering belief that we are recipients of God's intended life and peace, made possible through the finished work of Jesus Christ.

Ekron Malcolm

The emotional effects of fear can often lead to a sense of powerlessness and despair, as seen in Romans 7:24-25: "O wretched man that I am! Who shall deliver me from the body of this death? I thank God through Jesus Christ our Lord." These verses express the internal struggle and emotional anguish that fear can cause. Fear may make us feel wretched, but it is through Jesus Christ that we find deliverance and a path to emotional healing. His presence offers a way out of the despair that fear can bring into our lives.

Through a connection with Jesus, Christian believers discover a refuge that transcends the confines of fear. It is not merely an escape from the immediate discomfort but a total freedom and emotional restoration. Total deliverance is available through the power of Jesus Christ. It brings healing to wounds inflicted by fear and guides believers toward inner peace and resilience.

In the presence of Jesus, fear loses its paralyzing hold, making way for a newfound sense of strength and courage. His teachings and examples become a beacon, illuminating the path to emotional well-being. Instead of succumbing to the destructive nature of fear, Christians find solace and empowerment, ultimately leading to a life marked by faith, hope, and healing.

Breaking the Bondage to Fear

Chapter 2

Romans' Road to Courage

Romans 1:17, " For in it the righteousness of God is revealed from faith to faith; as it is written, 'The just shall live by faith.'"

In the previous chapter, we embarked on a journey to understand the complex nature of fear, recognizing that it can be both a protective instinct and a paralyzing force. As we dig deeper into our exploration of overcoming the spirit of fear, we will focus on specific passages that directly address fear and faith. These passages will serve as signposts along our road to courage.

To fully appreciate the wisdom contained within Romans, we must first understand its historical context. Paul wrote this letter to the Christians during a time of great uncertainty and upheaval. The Roman Empire was vast and diverse, and the early Christian community in Rome faced various challenges, including persecution, cultural clashes, and theological questions.

Romans is significant not only for its historical context but also for its profound theological insights. In this letter, Paul expounds on faith, grace, and righteousness. These themes are

Breaking the Bondage to Fear

woven throughout the text and provide a foundation for building our understanding of conquering fear through faith.

The Role of Faith

Faith is the key to salvation in Christ Jesus and the key to pleasing God. Believers are only received based on faith in Christ, which means that they come into salvation through accepting the Gospel's truth and the good news about the birth, death, and resurrection of Jesus. (Romans 10:17)

The book of Romans teaches that faith is the principle every Christian must live by. That faith comes through hearing the message of Christ and accepting it, believing it, living it by the power of the Spirit of Jesus, and trusting Him to guide us, which is paramount for success in our daily lives. (Romans 10:17)

To walk by faith means using God's word as our living rule. It also means acknowledging the truth of God's word and choosing not to lean on our limited understanding of life situations. First, we must realize how God expects us to act and then decide to obey such principles.

When we live by faith, we are saying, "God, You are right, and I trust what You say about how I should live." It also means trusting what His word says about who we are and what we can do. God's word, when believed, empowers us with great strength and decisive action.

Romans 1:17 is a foundational scripture that holds significant importance in understanding faith in the Christian context. "For in it the righteousness of God is revealed from faith to faith; as it is written, "The just shall live by faith." Righteousness is not based on human merit but is received as a gift through faith. The righteous are those who have been justified or declared righteous by God based on their trust in Him. By this faith, the righteous must continue to live and, in so doing, will please their Heavenly Father.

The phrase "from faith to faith" in this verse suggests a progression or a journey of faith. It implies that faith is not a one-time occurrence but a continuous and evolving process. As individuals grow in their faith, they gain a deeper and more profound understanding of God's righteousness. This progression fosters spiritual growth and maturation, highlighting the ongoing role of faith in the life of a believer.

Moreover, the verse cites the prophetic statement, "The just shall live by faith," which reinforces the concept that faith is not confined to a single act of belief but is a way of life for the righteous. It affirms that faith is the driving force behind the daily existence of those considered just in God's eyes. Faith is not merely a theological concept but a practical way of life and for following God's will.

Romans 1:17 emphasizes the central role of faith in the Christian journey. It highlights that God's righteousness is revealed through faith, a continuous and evolving process that serves as the foundation for the daily lives of every believer. Encouraging believers to rely on faith is the key to understanding and experiencing God's righteousness.

Breaking the Bondage to Fear

At its core, Romans emphasizes that faith is the key to salvation. Romans 3:22-24 states, "This righteousness is given through faith in Jesus Christ to all who believe. There is no difference between Jew and Gentile, for all have sinned and fall short of the glory of God, and all are justified freely by his grace through the redemption that came by Christ Jesus." (NIV)

Moreover, Romans clarifies that faith is not merely a passive belief but an active trust and reliance on God's promises. Romans chapter four provides an in-depth exploration of faith through the example of Abraham, the father of faith. It underscores that Abraham's unwavering faith in God's promises justified him, a powerful reminder of faith's transformative and life-altering impact.

The Book of Romans provides a profound theological exploration of the role of faith in the Christian tradition. It stresses faith in Christ Jesus as the means of salvation, emphasizes the active trust and reliance it entails, and links faith to righteousness and sanctification. Throughout its verses, Romans underscores the significance of faith as the cornerstone of the Christian walk, guiding believers on their journey of salvation and transformation.

Faith is the foundation of our relationship with God, the catalyst for transformation, and an antidote to fear. Through faith, we attain peace with God, renew our minds, and embrace our adoption into His family, effectively casting aside fear and embracing a life marked by courage and unwavering trust in our Heavenly Father.

Central Elements in Overcoming Fear

Ekron Malcolm

Faith is undeniably central to overcoming fear, and the Book of Romans provides profound insights into this powerful relationship. Romans 10:17 writes, " So then faith *comes* by hearing, and hearing by the word of God." This verse highlights the foundational role of faith, emphasizing that it is nurtured through the Word of God. When we immerse ourselves in Scripture and listen to His teachings, our faith grows stronger, enabling us to confront and conquer fear. Breaking down Romans 10:17 provides valuable insights into the transformative power of faith:

1. *Faith as a Dynamic Process:* The word "comes" in the verse suggests that faith is not a fixed state but a continuous process. It implies that faith can be cultivated and developed over time, evolving through our experiences and interactions with divine teachings.

2. *Hearing and Receiving the Word of God:* The verse emphasizes the importance of "hearing" in developing our faith. This goes beyond the physical act of auditory perception; it encompasses a deeper level of understanding and reception. It suggests that faith is not just a matter of superficially listening to words but involves a profound engagement with the divine message.

3. *The Word of God as the Source of Faith:* The verse highlights that faith is specifically nurtured "by the word of God." This underscores the significance of sacred scriptures, teachings, and divine revelations in shaping and reinforcing our faith. Immersing ourselves in the Word of God becomes a crucial means of establishing a connection with Jesus Christ and strengthening our trust and belief.

Breaking the Bondage to Fear

4. *Scripture as a Foundation for Confronting Fear:* The overall implication of the verse is that a strong foundation of faith, developed through an earnest engagement with the Word of God, equips us to confront and overcome fear. The teachings found in scripture provide guidance, reassurance, and a sense of purpose that can be instrumental in facing life's challenges with courage and conviction.

Romans 10:17 underscores faith's dynamic nature and highlights the importance of the word of God's teachings in its development. By actively engaging with the Word of God, we can cultivate a robust and resilient faith that is a powerful antidote to fear, enabling us to navigate life's uncertainties with confidence and trust in the divine plan.

Romans 4:20-21 offers an inspiring narrative about Abraham's unwavering faith: "He staggered not at the promise of God through unbelief but was strong in faith, giving glory to God, and being fully persuaded that what He had promised, He was able also to perform." Abraham's trust in God's promises allowed him to overcome fear and doubt. This passage reminds us that faith involves being fully convinced of God's ability to fulfill His promises, which, in turn, diminishes the grip of fear in our lives.

Living by faith means relying on God's promises, as Scripture reveals. It involves trusting in the assurances of God, such as forgiveness through Christ, the indwelling of the Holy Spirit, and the hope of eternal life. Faith, in this context, is an anchor in the unchanging promises of God. Faith-driven living involves seeking alignment with God's will. In living by faith, the righteous understand and follow God's desires for their lives. They seek His guidance, obey His commands, and participate in His redemptive plan.

Romans 5:1-2 beautifully illustrates the relationship between faith and peace: "Therefore being justified by faith, we have peace with God through our Lord Jesus Christ. By whom also we have access by faith into this grace wherein we stand and rejoice in the hope of the glory of God." This passage reminds us that faith leads to justification and peace with God. Such peace is an antidote to fear, offering a serene and hopeful perspective that can overcome life's anxieties. His peace, when applied, shields against fear, instilling confidence in God's promises and steadfast love.

In Romans 12:21, the Apostle Paul encourages believers, saying, "Be not overcome of evil, but overcome evil with good." This verse emphasizes the importance of faith in choosing goodness and love over fear and evil. By firmly believing in God's goodness and His ability to overcome evil, we can confront fear and negativity in our lives with faith as our guiding light, promoting acts of love and kindness as we choose to overcome fear and darkness.

As we journey along Romans' road to courage, we will continuously reference and draw inspiration from the book's teachings. We aim to uncover the transformative power of faith, as exemplified in the concept of adoption, and to use this understanding as a foundation for conquering fear. As we continue this transformative journey, we will discover the freedom that comes from embracing the Spirit of adoption and faith.

Breaking the Bondage to Fear

Chapter 3

The Spirit of Adoption

Romans 8:15, "For you did not receive the spirit of bondage again to fear, but you received the Spirit of adoption by whom we cry out, 'Abba Father.'"

Fear vs. Adoption

At the heart of Romans 8:15 lies another great truth—the contrast between the spirit of bondage, which leads to fear, and the Spirit of adoption, which ushers in freedom and a relationship with God. This verse summarises the essence of our journey to conquer fear through faith.

As we explore the concept of the Spirit of adoption in-depth, we will consider what it means to be adopted sons and daughters of God and how this life-changing truth can free us from the bondage to fear.

Breaking the Bondage to Fear

The Spirit of adoption gives us a deep sense of belonging and security. It reassures us that we are not alone in our struggles and have a loving Heavenly Father who cares for us. This knowledge can be a powerful antidote to the fear of abandonment or isolation.

The passage in Romans 8:15 also highlights the intimate relationship we can have with God as we cry out to Him, addressing Him as "Abba, Father." This personal connection with God strengthens our faith and provides us with a feeling of comfort and protection.

Romans 8:15 tells us, "For ye have not received the spirit of bondage again to fear, but ye have received the Spirit of adoption, whereby we cry, 'Abba, Father.'"

Indeed, the statement highlights the concept of bondage and its implications, mainly focusing on the control exerted by fear. When we talk about being in bondage to something, it signifies a state of being controlled or dominated by a particular force. In this context, the scripture in Romans 15 is referenced, suggesting that being under the sway of fear essentially enslaves a person. This mental enslavement is what happens to many who are Christians, yet our position in Christ is freedom, but the devil wields his deception to try and keep Christians in bondage to fear, which is a state of mental slavery.

According to Romans 15, when fear takes control, it operates as a master over an individual, rendering them a slave to its influence. This enslavement goes beyond mere apprehension; it extends to the point where a person's thoughts, actions, and emotions are constrained by anxiety, often leading to a sense of hopelessness. In such a state, individuals are not free to fully live, express themselves, or pursue their potential because fear dictates their choices and responses.

The message draws a sharp contrast by introducing the liberating influence of Christ. Through a relationship with Christ, one is set free from the bondage to fear and is liberated in the hope of His adoption. The mention of freedom from the fear of death, hell, and the grave implies a profound transformation. In Christianity, the belief in and the confession of Christ's sacrifice and resurrection provides eternal life, eliminating the fear of what comes after death.

This liberation made possible through Christ, is not just a theoretical concept; it signifies a tangible release from the paralyzing grip of fear. It opens the door to a life lived without constant anxiety and the despair associated with being enslaved to the spirit of fear. In essence, the message suggests that through faith in Christ, individuals can experience a newfound freedom that empowers them to live life more abundantly and without the constraints imposed by fear.

Before fully appreciating the Spirit of adoption, we must understand its contrast with the spirit of slavery. The spirit of slavery represents bondage, fear, and a sense of powerlessness. It's the belief that we are at the mercy of our circumstances and alone in facing life's challenges.

1. The Spirit of Bondage: The "spirit of bondage" refers to a state of enslavement, fear, and powerlessness. It symbolizes the

Breaking the Bondage to Fear

condition of being bound by sin, living under the weight of guilt, and feeling separated from God. In this context, bondage implies a life marked by the inability to break free from the chains of sin, the fear of divine judgment, and a sense of isolation from God's love and grace.

2. Fear and Powerlessness: Fear dominates under the spirit of bondage. This fear is not merely the apprehension of punishment but also the anxiety of being abandoned and left to navigate life's challenges alone. The individual under this spirit may feel overwhelmed, lacking the confidence and assurance to face life's uncertainties. It reflects a mindset not aligned with the freedom offered through Christ.

3. Freedom from Fear: The Spirit of adoption dispels fear and replaces it with the security of knowing one's place in God's family. Adopted children in Roman society were granted full rights and privileges within their new family; similarly, believers are granted access to the inheritance and promises of God. This assurance breaks the chains of fear, affirming that they are no longer enslaved to fear but heirs, co-heirs with Christ Jesus (Romans 8:17).

Romans 8:15 is a powerful reminder of the radical transformation that occurs in the life of a believer. It underlines the shift from a spirit of bondage and fear to the liberating Spirit of adoption, wherein believers find a new identity, intimacy with God, and freedom from the shackles of sin and uncertainty. This transformation is not merely a change in legal standing but a profound reorientation of the believer's heart and relationship with the Father.

Ekron Malcolm

One of the most touching aspects of Romans 8:15 is the understanding that, through the Spirit of adoption, we can cry out to God as "Abba! Father!" This cry reflects an intimate relationship with God characterized by trust, love, and a deep connection. The Spirit of adoption offers us freedom from fear in various ways.

The Sense of Belonging & Security

Knowing we are adopted into God's family is a source of strength, belonging and security. We find a beautiful depiction of this concept in Romans 8:15; faith in Christ means we are no longer bound by fear or insecurity. Instead, we are welcomed into God's family as adopted children, finding our place in His love and grace; it reassures us that we no longer have to dread the agony of rejection or the pain of abandonment. In God's family, we discover unwavering security and a love that endures all.

Our Heavenly Father's care for us transcends human understanding, offering love and concern beyond measure. Romans 8:28 reminds us of this reassuring truth: "And we know that all things work together for good to them that love God, to them who are the called according to his purpose." This verse speaks to the divine care that God exercises in our lives. Even in the face of uncertainty and fear, we can rest assured that He orchestrates all things for our good. This fatherly care is an anchor in the storm of life, giving us the strength to face our fears head-on.

Romans 8:38-39 goes even deeper into the idea of God's unwavering care: "For I am persuaded that neither death, nor life, nor

Breaking the Bondage to Fear

angels, nor principalities, nor powers, nor things present, nor things to come, nor height, nor depth, nor any other creature, shall be able to separate us from the love of God, which is in Christ Jesus our Lord." This passage emphasizes the immensity of God's love and its capacity to transcend every possible fear or threat. It assures us that nothing in the entire universe, neither our past nor our future, can separate us from His love. In this incredible love, we find the ultimate source of our security.

Our Heavenly Father's care is not limited to our spiritual well-being alone but extends to our earthly needs. In Matthew 6:26, Jesus tells us, "Behold the fowls of the air: for they sow not, neither do they reap, nor gather into barns; yet your heavenly Father feedeth them. Are ye not much better than they?" This verse shows us that God's care extends to even the minor details of our lives. Just as He provides for the birds, His care for us is evident in the abundance of His provisions, offering further comfort and security in times of fear.

Romans 15:13 reminds us of our hope and security in our Heavenly Father's care: "Now the God of hope fill you with all joy and peace in believing, that ye may abound in hope, through the power of the Holy Ghost." The God of hope fills us with joy and peace through faith in Him. In this divine partnership, we experience a profound sense of security, even in fear, knowing He is the source of our hope and strength.

Romans 8:15 captures the essence of the Christian faith, emphasizing the believers' profound relationship with God through the Spirit of adoption. Let's go deeper into the significance of this

Ekron Malcolm

verse and explore how it resonates with the themes of trust, love, connection, and freedom from fear.

Breaking the Bondage to Fear

1. Spirit of Adoption: The concept of adoption is central to understanding the relationship between believers and God. In the context of Romans 8:15, it signifies that through the work of the Holy Spirit, believers are not merely servants or followers but are adopted into God's family. This adoption implies God's deliberate and unconditional choice to make believers His children.

2. Crying Out as "Abba! Father!": Using the term "Abba" adds a layer of intimacy and warmth to the relationship. "Abba" is an Aramaic term for father that conveys a sense of familiarity and closeness. The fact that believers can cry out to God using such an intimate term reflects a level of trust and comfort beyond a formal or distant relationship.

3. Intimate Relationship with God: The cry of "Abba! Father!" reflects a deeply personal and intimate connection with God. It goes beyond acknowledging God's existence or a distant admiration. Instead, it portrays a relationship characterized by mutual love, trust, and understanding. In this intimate connection, believers can approach God with vulnerability, knowing He embraces them as cherished children.

4. Trust: Trust is a fundamental element of any meaningful relationship. Through the Spirit of adoption, believers can trust God as a loving and caring Father. This trust is built on the assurance that God's love is unwavering, and His plans are for the well-being of His children. The cry of "Abba! Father!" declares reliance on God's faithfulness and goodness.

5. Love: The Spirit of adoption manifests God's profound love for humanity. By adopting believers into His family, God expresses a love transcending human comprehension. This love is not based on merit but is an outpouring of God's grace and mercy. The cry of "Abba! Father!" responds to an acknowledgment of this overwhelming love.

6. Deep Connection: The relationship described in Romans 8:15 is not a superficial or transactional one. It is a deep and meaningful connection that surpasses earthly relationships. The Spirit of adoption creates a spiritual bond between God and believers that goes beyond the limitations of human understanding, providing a sense of belonging and identity.

7. Freedom from Fear: The verse highlights that the Spirit of adoption liberates believers from fear. This freedom is multi-faceted:

Freedom from the fear of rejection: Believers can approach God without the fear of being cast aside, knowing they are accepted as His children.

Freedom from the fear of condemnation: The assurance of God's love dispels the fear of judgment, fostering a sense of security in the relationship.

Freedom from the fear of the unknown: Trust in God as a loving Father alleviates anxieties about the future, knowing His plans are for good.

Romans 8:15 is a powerful reminder of the radical transformation that occurs in the life of a believer. It highlights the shift from a spirit of bondage and fear to the liberating Spirit of adoption, wherein believers find a new identity, intimacy with God, and freedom from the shackles of sin and uncertainty. This transformation is not merely a change in legal standing but a profound

Breaking the Bondage to Fear

reorientation of the believer's heart and relationship with the Father.

These spiritual truths are a foundation on which we can build our lives, offering hope, comfort, and unwavering security as we confront the challenges and fears of the world and the attacks from the realm of darkness.

Knowing that we are adopted into God's family gives us a sense of belonging and security. We no longer have to fear rejection or abandonment. When we fully embrace the Spirit of adoption, we trust that our Father has a divine plan for our lives. This trust replaces the fear of the unknown with a sense of purpose and direction.

We sincerely embrace the Spirit of adoption and His power to transform our lives. We have learned that it is possible to transition from a life dominated by fear to one characterized by faith and courage. The message of Romans 8:15 will remain a guiding light as we explore the transformative power of faith and the path to becoming conquerors in Christ.

Ekron Malcolm

Prayer of Thankfulness

Heavenly Father, I come before You with a grateful heart, overwhelmed by Your love and mercy. Thank You for the immeasurable gift of adoption into Your family through Jesus Christ, my Lord and Savior.

In awe of Your love, I recognize that I was once lost, but You, in Your infinite compassion, saw fit to bring me into Your family. Through the sacrifice of Jesus, You opened the gates of adoption, welcoming me as Your beloved child. I am humbled by the fact that You chose me to be a part of Your family.

As I reflect on the significance of this adoption, I am filled with a profound sense of belonging and security. I no longer need to fear rejection or abandonment, for I now stand firmly under the shelter of Your love. Your embrace embodies unconditional love and the assurance that I am never alone, even in my darkest hours.

I thank You for this adoption's hope and joy in my life. It is a living testament to Your boundless grace and unfailing love. In times of doubt and fear, I find solace in knowing that I am Your child, and You are my Heavenly Father, guiding me with wisdom and tenderness.

Heavenly Father, I express my deepest gratitude for being adopted into Your family. I acknowledge the sacrifice of Your Son, Jesus Christ, who made it possible for me to experience this

Breaking the Bondage to Fear

incredible love and mercy. I will carry this truth in my heart, living as a testament to Your grace and love, and I choose to reflect Your love onto others, sharing the good news of salvation in Jesus' name, I pray. Amen.

Ekron Malcolm

Chapter 4

Walking in Victory

Romans 8:28, "And we know that all things work together for good to them that love God, to them who are the called according to his purpose."

Fear often thrives when we perceive ourselves as powerless or defeated. However, a victorious mindset is an antidote to such fear. A victorious mindset will help us understand the significance of adopting a victorious attitude and faith's pivotal role in its development.

Victory is not merely a destination but a state of mind—a perspective that shapes our attitudes, decisions, and actions. It's the inner assurance that we can overcome challenges and emerge stronger regardless of circumstances. Walking in victory involves practical steps and intentional choices that empower us to conquer fear. Here are some strategies that lead to a victorious mindset:

Ekron Malcolm

Embracing The Power of Faith

Faith is unequivocally presented as the cornerstone of victory in the book of Romans. It is not merely a passive belief but an unwavering conviction in God's promises and the assurance that He stands by our side in all circumstances. This concept underlines the profound truth that faith is not just a spiritual abstraction but a powerful force that fuels our triumph over adversity. The Apostle Paul writes in Romans 8:28, "And we know that all things work together for good to them that love God, to them who are the called according to his purpose." This verse reinforces the understanding that faith is the foundation for victory, for it embodies the absolute trust that God's providence will guide us to triumph even in the face of life's most daunting challenges.

Faith gives us the strength and courage to confront adversity in a world of uncertainty and trials. By anchoring our faith in the unchanging character of God, we find a firm foundation on which to stand, a source of enduring hope amidst the storms of life. Romans 4:20-21 illustrates this beautifully: "He staggered not at the promise of God through unbelief, but was strong in faith, giving glory to God; And being fully persuaded that, what he had promised, he was able also to perform." Just as Abraham's unwavering faith in God's promises led to victory, so too can our steadfast trust in God's unchanging nature assure us of triumph in our lives.

The teachings of Romans emphasize that faith is not a mere accessory in the journey of life but the very cornerstone of victory. The unwavering belief in God's promises and the assurance of His constant presence allows us to confront adversity boldly. Through

Breaking the Bondage to Fear

faith, we find the strength to navigate life's challenges, confident in our Creator's unchanging character. As we anchor our faith in God, we discover that it is the key to enduring victory in a world where trials and tribulations abound.

Resilience in the Face of Setbacks

Life's journey is replete with setbacks and trials that challenge our resolve and test our inner strength. In these trying moments, resilience emerges as an essential attribute for surviving and thriving in adversity. Fortunately, the teachings of Romans provide us with a spiritual roadmap for building resilience. By drawing from the divine wisdom of this biblical book, we can cultivate the mental and emotional fortitude needed to bounce back from life's most daunting challenges.

Romans teaches us that we find growth and transformation opportunities in adversity. Just as gold is refined in the fire, our faith is strengthened through trials and tribulations. Romans 5:3-4 reminds us, "We glory in tribulations also: knowing that tribulation worketh patience; And patience, experience; and experience, hope." Resilience is not simply about enduring hardships but using them as stepping stones toward a brighter future. In the face of setbacks, the book of Romans encourages us to embrace adversity as a catalyst for spiritual growth and character development.

Moreover, Romans instills in us the unwavering hope that adversity is not the end of the road but a chapter in our life's journey. Romans 8:28 declares, "And we know that all things work together for good to them that love God, to them who are the called according to his purpose." This powerful assurance reminds us that even in the most challenging circumstances, there is a more excellent divine plan at work, and our setbacks are instrumental in shaping us for the purpose God has ordained. This teaching fuels our resilience, for we understand that our trials are part of a grander narrative, and with faith, perseverance, and a resilient spirit, we can emerge from setbacks with newfound strength and a victorious mindset.

Renewing the Mind

Renewing the mind is a central theme in the teachings of Romans, and it plays a crucial role in achieving victory in our lives. This transformation involves a fundamental shift in our thought patterns, compelling us to re-evaluate our perspectives and align them with the principles of faith. As the Apostle Paul urges in Romans 12:2, "And be not conformed to this world: but be ye transformed by the renewing of your mind, that ye may prove what is that good, and acceptable, and perfect, will of God." It is essential to renew the mind to discern and fulfill the divine will, ultimately leading to a life characterized by triumph over adversity.

Renewing the mind is not a superficial or casual endeavour but an intentional process. It calls for a continuous examination of our thought patterns and a commitment to shedding the world's influences that may lead us astray from the path of faith. Doing so creates space for the indwelling of God's transformative truth and wisdom. Romans teaches us that this renewal is a catalyst for achieving victory because it equips us with the discernment to recognize what is truly good, acceptable, and perfect in the eyes of God. By aligning our thoughts with these divine standards, we are better equipped to navigate the challenges and adversities of life.

Breaking the Bondage to Fear

The teachings of Romans emphasize the importance of renewing the mind, which is crucial for our journey to success. It requires intentionally shifting our thought patterns from worldly influences to faith-based principles. The truth in Romans 12:2 is a guiding light, prompting us to undergo this transformation, to understand and live according to God's perfect will. When we renew our minds, we become better equipped to face the pressures of the evil one and life's challenges. As a result, we can live a life that reflects divine purposes and leads to triumphant living.

Renewing our minds is crucial to developing a confident outlook on God's plan for our lives. It is an essential ingredient of a victorious mindset. As we commit to transforming our thinking patterns, we realize that having faith allows us to trust in God's sovereign orchestration of our life's journey. This trust remains unwavering even when we face uncertainty because we understand that every experience, challenge, and opportunity is part of God's purposeful design.

As we encounter the uncertainties and difficulties of life, we recognize that God is working to create a beautiful and meaningful story out of our experiences. This knowledge gives us the strength to face challenges with determination, knowing they lead us toward a divine purpose. The book of Romans shows us that by having faith and renewing our minds, we can align ourselves with God's great plan and move forward confidently in His purpose.

Renewing our minds is crucial in nurturing our confidence in God's plan for our lives. This transformation of thought patterns through faith is the foundation of a successful mindset. We discover a wellspring of inner strength and confidence by embracing uncertainty and trusting that God is orchestrating a purposeful journey for us. By renewing our minds, we can find clarity and assurance in God's divine design, ultimately leading to a purposeful and victorious life.

Biblical Examples of Victory

Let us take an in-depth look at the story of Abraham before he became the father of many nations.

"After this, the word of the LORD came to Abram in a vision: 'Do not be afraid, Abram. I am your shield, your very great reward.' But Abram said, 'Sovereign LORD, what can you give me since I remain childless and the one who will inherit my estate is Eliezer of Damascus?' And Abram said, 'You have given me no children; so a servant in my household will be my heir.'

Then the word of the LORD came to him: 'This man will not be your heir, but a son who is your own flesh and blood will be your heir.' He took him outside and said, 'Look up at the sky and count the stars—if indeed you can count them.' Then he said to him, 'So shall your offspring be.'

Abram believed the LORD, and he credited it to him as righteousness."
(Genesis 15:1-6)

Abraham, initially known as Abram, faced a deep-seated fear and concern regarding his lack of an heir. In that time's cultural and historical context, having a son and heir was of utmost importance.

Breaking the Bondage to Fear

It was not just a matter of personal fulfillment but also a critical aspect of inheritance, legacy, and the promise God had given him.

Abram had received a promise from God that he would be the father of a great nation. However, as the years passed and he and his wife Sarai remained childless, doubt and fear began to creep into Abram's heart. The concern about not having an heir to fulfill God's promise was a natural human reaction, especially given the societal expectations and the significance placed on lineage.

God's response to Abram's fear is a powerful reassurance of His faithfulness and a reminder of the magnitude of the promise. The phrase "Do not be afraid, Abram. I am your shield, your very great reward" underscores God's commitment to Abram's well-being and emphasizes that God Himself is the ultimate reward.

Abram, though, expresses his apprehension, questioning what God could give him since he remained childless. In proposing that Eliezer of Damascus might become his heir, Abram was considering the cultural practice of adopting a servant as an heir when one lacked a natural heir. However, God intervenes to clarify that it would not be through a servant but through a son of Abram's flesh and blood that the promise would be fulfilled.

To strengthen Abram's faith, God takes him outside and instructs him to count the stars, using the vastness of the night sky as a metaphor for the multitude of Abram's descendants. This visual representation was meant to expand Abram's perspective beyond the immediate circumstances and instill a sense of the grandeur of God's promise.

Ekron Malcolm

The crucial turning point in this narrative is Abram's response—he believed the Lord. Despite the apparent impossibility of the situation, Abram trusted in God's promise. This act of faith is highlighted in the concluding statement: "He [God] credited it to him [Abram] as righteousness." This implies that Abram's faith was accounted as righteousness in the eyes of God.

Abram's journey from fear and doubt to faith is an example of the challenges and victories inherent in a life of faith when we put our trust in God's promises, even when circumstances seem insurmountable. Abraham, later known as the father of faith, becomes a central figure in the biblical narrative, and his story serves as an inspiration for believers to trust in God's faithfulness even in the face of uncertainty.

God's words to Abram were a source of comfort and assurance, dispelling his fear and instilling peace. Trusting in God's promises is a means to overcome the grip of fear and experience victory.

1. Divine Reassurance:
   God addresses Abram's fear directly, saying, "Do not be afraid, Abram." This divine reassurance immediately acknowledges Abram's emotional state and seeks to calm his troubled mind. The declaration "I am your shield, your exceedingly great reward" shows God's nature as a protector and highlights the ultimate satisfaction of being in a relationship with Him. By assuring Abram of His presence and care, God provides a foundation for dispelling fear.

2. Identification of Concerns:

Breaking the Bondage to Fear

God reassures Abram and allows him to express his concerns openly. Abram voices his worry about remaining childless and the potential heir being a servant. God's willingness to engage in this conversation demonstrates His understanding of human emotions and concerns. Sometimes, the mere act of expressing fears can begin dispelling them.

3. Clarification of the Promise:
   God does not leave Abram in uncertainty. He clarifies that the heir will not be Eliezer but a son from Abram's flesh and blood. This specificity in God's response removes ambiguity and reinforces the reliability of the promise. Clarity in God's communication is a powerful antidote to fear, providing a solid foundation for building trust.

4. Visual Representation:
   God takes Abram outside and instructs him to look at the stars, using a tangible and awe-inspiring visual representation to convey the magnitude of the promise. This exercise serves as a vivid reminder of God's unlimited power and the vastness of His plans.

5. Abram's Act of Faith:
   The turning point in this narrative is Abram's decision to believe God despite the seemingly impossible circumstances. His trust in God's promises becomes an active choice, shifting his focus from fear to faith. As mentioned in the scripture, this act of faith is credited to him as righteousness. It illustrates that trusting in God's promises is not

merely a passive acknowledgment but an intentional decision to anchor one's life in God's truth.

Abram's encounter with God in Genesis 15 demonstrates how God's words, reassurance, clarity, and visual representation worked together to dispel fear. Trusting in God's promises became the pathway to peace and victory over the spirit of fear, showcasing the profound impact of faith in overcoming life's challenges. We are forever encouraged as believers to lean on the promises of God, finding solace, peace, and victory in Him.

Abraham's unwavering faith is a beacon of inspiration in the book of Romans. Despite his old age and the impossibility of bearing children, Abraham believed in God's promise of many descendants. His steadfast faith allowed him to remain firm in believing the promise from God that he would have a son who would eventually inherit his legacy of being the father of the Israelite nation. Abraham's victorious mindset was focused on the fulfillment of this promise, and his remarkable journey of faith serves as a timeless example of trust and obedience. His life demonstrates that faith, even in the face of daunting circumstances, can turn barrenness into fruitfulness and uncertainty into a legacy of faith for generations to come.

The story of Paul, formerly known as Saul, is another compelling testament to the transformative power of faith. Saul was an ardent persecutor of Christians, consumed by a zealous, misguided mindset. However, a life-altering encounter with Christ on the road to Damascus led to his conversion and a radical transformation. In Romans, Paul shares his experiences and the shift in his beliefs and values. His unwavering faith in Christ as the Saviour

Breaking the Bondage to Fear

and his newfound commitment to spreading the Gospel became the driving force behind his life's purpose. Despite facing immense trials, including imprisonment and persecution, Paul's victorious mindset enabled him to impact the world with his teachings and writings, leaving an enduring legacy of faith and spiritual transformation.

These two stories from the Book of Romans highlight the extraordinary capacity of faith to bring about personal transformation and to inspire others to do the same. Abraham's faith shows us that no situation is beyond the reach of God's promises, and Paul's transformation shows us the power of faith to reshape our values and purpose in life. Through their stories, we discover that a victorious mindset, rooted in unwavering faith, can lead to a life marked by purpose, resilience, and a lasting legacy.

Remember that walking in victory is a continuous journey, not a one-time achievement. Victory is not the absence of challenges but the presence of unwavering faith through it all. Victory is not a distant dream; it's a journey illuminated by faith and a journey we can all embark upon as we become conquerors in Christ.

Ekron Malcolm

Prayers of Faith and Commitment

Dear Heavenly Father, I come before You with a heart full of gratitude for Your abundant grace and boundless love. I thank You for the promise of Your Word, which assures me that as I renew my mind through Your teachings, I can become resilient and steadfast in my faith, nurturing a victorious mindset that overcomes all challenges.

Thank You for always being there for me and for Your unconditional love and guidance. Help me to remain steadfast in my faith and to always trust in Your plan for my life.

Lord, I commit myself to this transforming journey, seeking a renewal of my mind through the wisdom and truths in Your Word. I acknowledge that I need Your guidance to navigate life's complexities and to align my thought patterns with Your divine purpose. Grant me the strength and wisdom to consistently immerse myself in Your Word so that I may grow in faith and find the resilience to withstand the trials that come my way.

Help me, Father, to maintain an unwavering trust in Your promises, just as Your Word encourages. May my faith in You be the cornerstone of my life, allowing me to confidently face adversity with the assurance that You are always with me. Grant me the grace to develop and maintain a victorious mindset that empowers me to shine as a testimony of Your glory to those around me.

Breaking the Bondage to Fear

I thank You for the transforming power of faith and the promise of victory in the name of Jesus Christ, my Lord and Saviour. Amen.

Ekron Malcolm

Chapter 5

Embracing God's Love to Conquer Fear

Romans 8:38-39, "For I am persuaded, that neither death, nor life, nor angels, nor principalities, nor powers, nor things present, nor things to come, nor height, nor depth, nor any other creature, shall be able to separate us from the love of God, which is in Christ Jesus our Lord."

In our pursuit of breaking the bondage to fear, we arrive at a evolutionary truth—the power of God's love as the ultimate antidote to fear. This chapter explores the profound teachings within Romans and the broader context of the Bible that reveal the supremacy of love over fear.

The Apostle Paul reminds us of the overarching role of love in his writings. In 1 Corinthians 13:13, he states, " And now these three remain: faith, hope and love. But the greatest of these is love." (NIV). This foundational verse underscores that love is the pinnacle of Christian virtues and a powerful force against fear.

Throughout the book of Romans, we find echoes of God's love as a transforming agent, revealed most profoundly through

Jesus Christ: Romans 5:8, "But God commendeth his love toward us, in that, while we were yet sinners, Christ died for us."

This verse highlights the sacrificial nature of God's love as revealed through the crucifixion of Jesus Christ. It emphasizes that God's love is not conditional; it extends to us even in our brokenness and sin. The cross becomes the ultimate symbol of God's love, demonstrating that He gave His Son for our redemption.

Romans 8:38-39 - "For I am persuaded, that neither death, nor life, nor angels, nor principalities, nor powers, nor things present, nor things to come, nor height, nor depth, nor any other creature, shall be able to separate us from the love of God, which is in Christ Jesus our Lord." This powerful passage recounts the unfailing nature of God's love as revealed through Jesus Christ. It assures us that nothing—no fear, no circumstance—can separate us from the love of God, which is manifested in Christ.

Romans 13:10 - "Love worketh no ill to his neighbour: therefore love is the fulfilling of the law." Love's role in fulfilling God's law is revealed in Christ's relationship to His Father. We reflect on how Jesus Christ embodied this love through His teachings, compassion for all, and ultimate sacrifice. His life on earth exemplified love as the highest expression of righteousness.

Choosing God's Love Over Fear

In our pursuit to conquer fear and embrace God's love as the ultimate remedy, we turn to 1 John 4:18 for guidance. This verse declares that perfect love casts out all fear. It reminds us that God's

Breaking the Bondage to Fear

love, perfectly revealed through Jesus Christ, has the power to dispel even the most pervasive fears that haunt our minds. With this understanding, we confront the crippling fear of inadequacy, the paralyzing fear of rejection, and the condemning fear that we are unworthy of love. In Jesus, we find the embodiment of perfect love to cast out all these fears from our lives. In Jesus, the embodiment of perfect love underscores the idea that Jesus is the ultimate representation of unconditional and selfless love. This portrayal implies a divine and exemplary standard of love that goes beyond human comprehension, suggesting a source of inspiration and aspiration.

Our Lord Jesus is a model for us to follow. His life and teachings provide a tangible example of embodying love, compassion, and forgiveness. By observing and understanding the actions of Jesus, individuals are encouraged to emulate these qualities in their own lives.

Moreover, the statement suggests that Jesus sets an example and gives us the means to cast out all these fears from our lives. This indicates that recognizing and accepting Jesus's perfect love offers a powerful tool for breaking the bondage to fear. The implication is that faith in Jesus and a deep understanding of His love can be a powerful force, enabling individuals to confront and conquer their anxieties and fears.

In essence, the statement conveys a message of hope, encouragement, and empowerment, suggesting that embracing the love embodied in Jesus can lead to a life free from the shackles of fear and insecurity.

Ekron Malcolm

Trusting in God's love, as illuminated by the life and teachings of Jesus Christ, becomes crucial, especially when faced with life's most challenging moments. Like a child who places unwavering faith in a loving parent's care, we can confidently rely on God's unfailing love to protect us in times of danger, comfort us in times of sadness, and guide us in times of uncertainty. This trust in God's love gives us peace of mind and empowers us to stand firm in the face of fear, knowing that we are not alone, and that the very essence of love surrounds us. Trusting in God's love as revealed through Jesus Christ is a powerful source of strength and comfort that dispels the devil's lies. God's love is a force more potent than any fear-inducing deception. Trusting in God's love is necessary to dispel the lies of the devil, which often manifest as fear and anxiety. This trust becomes a source of inner peace, strength, and empowerment, allowing us as believers to face life's challenges with courage and resilience, secure in the knowledge that we are enveloped in the unending and unconditional love of Jesus Christ.

Trusting in God's love, especially during life's most challenging circumstances, is extremely important. We can be assured that nothing can separate us from the love of God, which serves as an unshakable foundation of our faith. This biblical truth becomes a beacon of hope when we struggle with loss, pain, or uncertainty in times of adversity. It reminds us that no matter how difficult the situation may seem, God's love remains constant and unwavering. We find comfort in knowing His love transcends the temporal and the physical and encompasses even the spiritual realms. Trusting in God's love in such moments empowers us to face adversity with courage and unwavering faith. We know we are not alone, and His love sustains us.

Breaking the Bondage to Fear

Ekron Malcolm

Prayer to Cultivate God's Love

Dear Heavenly Father, I come before You with my heart open and humbled, seeking to embrace the boundless love You graciously offer. As I reflect on the example set by Your Son, Jesus Christ, I'm reminded of the profound truth that Your perfect love can cast out all fear. I yearn to cultivate this love in my life, to be a vessel of Your light in a world often shrouded in darkness.

Lord, help me to truly understand the depth of Your love, as revealed through the life and teachings of Jesus. And grant me the wisdom and power to conquer the fears of inadequacy, rejection, or condemnation. I choose now to trust in Your unwavering love, just as a child trusts in the care of a loving parent. I believe I am accepted in the beloved of Jesus Christ.

Teach me to live a life characterized by love, mirroring the example set by Jesus. Help me to shift my focus from self-concern to genuine care for others so that I may become an instrument of Your love in a world yearning for compassion and grace. As I walk this path, I carry Your love in my heart, dispelling fear's grip not only in my own life but in the lives of those I touch.

Father, I surrender myself to Your love, seeking to align with Your perfect will and to reflect Your light. May Your love fill me to the brim, casting out fear, and may I, in turn, become a beacon of Your love, sharing it with a world in desperate need. In the name of Your beloved Son, Jesus Christ, I pray. Amen.

Breaking the Bondage to Fear

Chapter 6

The Art of Christian Meditation

Romans 12:2, "And be not conformed to this world: but be ye transformed by the renewing of your mind, that ye may prove what is that good, and acceptable, and perfect, will of God."

Romans 12:2 is an essential foundational scripture to help Christians break the bondage to fear. In this verse, the Apostle Paul emphasizes the importance of a mental transformation, urging believers to avoid conforming to the patterns and values of the secular world. Instead, he urges them to renew their minds and be transformed by the power of God.

Dwelling on God's Word

Christian meditation involves meditating on God's Word, contemplating His promises, and internalizing His teachings. The act of practicing is closely connected to the process of renewing one's mind, which is a fundamental aspect of Romans 12:2. By meditating on the Scriptures, we intentionally redirect our attention away from the negative influences and thought patterns of

Breaking the Bondage to Fear

the world and instead immerse ourselves in the truth and wisdom of God.

Meditating on God's Word reshapes our thought processes, helping us replace fear and anxiety with faith and confidence. This renewal of the mind empowers us to think, react, and respond differently to the challenges and fears we encounter in life.

Christian meditation helps us to align our thoughts with God's will. By meditating on His Word, we can understand His purpose and plan for our lives, which often involve overcoming fear and finding courage in Him. Aligning our thoughts with God's will enables us to make choices that align with His desires for us, resulting in a life of faith and confidence.

Romans 12:2 instructs us to practice Christian meditation to transform our minds and, as a result, our lives. By engaging in this practice, we can break free from the world's fear-driven patterns and adopt a renewed perspective anchored in God's promises and unwavering love. Through this renewal process, we can conquer fear and approach life's challenges with confidence and faith.

Christian meditation is a practice that encourages believers not to skim the surface of Scripture but to ponder and muse on the Word of God deeply. As Christians, daily meditation on God's Word is a vital spiritual discipline that can profoundly impact our lives and help us conquer fear. Meditating on God's Word is essential for spiritual growth, understanding, and courage. Joshua 1:8 states, "Keep this Book of the Law always on your lips; meditate on it day and night, so that you may be careful to do everything written in it. Then you will be prosperous and successful." (NIV)

Joshua 1:8 highlights the importance of keeping the Book of the Law close to us and meditating on it continually. Meditating on God's Word will fill our minds with divine truths that can counter doubts and anxieties rooted in fear. Constantly having God's teachings and promises in our thoughts will provide a foundation of faith to help us combat the spirit of fear. By following this guidance, we can find the courage to face life's challenges with the assurance that God's wisdom and guidance are with us. Reflecting on divine teachings consistently serves as a reminder of God's guidance and wisdom. It enables us to internalize the values and principles in the Scriptures and make them an integral part of our lives. Doing so makes us better equipped to navigate life's challenges with a firm moral compass.

When we delight in God's law and meditate on it day and night, we are blessed (Psalm 1:2). This constant meditation is a mental exercise and a spiritual practice that nurtures a deep connection with the Lord Jesus Christ. Through regular reflection on God's Word, Christians can find solace and guidance in times of confusion and distress. Each verse reveals new insights into the spiritual journey, enriching the experience with every meditation.

Psalm 1:2 further highlights that those who delight in the law of the Lord and meditate on it day and night find true joy and stability in their faith. Fear often arises from uncertainty and insecurity, but also the devil often uses those times to magnify the spirit of fear in our lives. Meditating on God's Word brings a sense of grounding and security. It reminds Christians of the

Breaking the Bondage to Fear

unchanging nature of God's promises and His unshakable love. This knowledge can be a powerful antidote to the crippling effects of the spirit of fear.

Meditation on God's Word is a valuable source of wisdom and insight for believers. It helps us to differentiate between right and wrong, make morally sound decisions, and find inner peace during life's difficulties. By aligning our thoughts with God's teachings, we can lead a life that reflects His will and purpose, which in turn leads to prosperity and success, as stated in Joshua 1:8. Success in a spiritual sense is not just about material wealth; it's about living a life full of purpose, peace, and fulfillment.

Moreover, meditation on God's Word enables us to shift our focus away from fear-inducing thoughts towards thoughts that inspire hope and courage. The mind is a powerful instrument, and by filling it with God's promises and the lessons from Scripture, Christians are better equipped to combat the negative thought patterns that often accompany fear. This transformation of the mind is a vital step in overcoming the spirit of fear.

Meditating on God's Word can provide a sense of purpose and direction in the face of fear. It helps believers discern God's will and find solace amid uncertainty. This sense of purpose can empower us to confront our fears with resilience and determination, knowing God's wisdom guides us.

Furthermore, meditation on God's Word does provide comfort and encouragement during times of fear and adversity. The Scriptures contain countless stories of individuals who faced fear and trials but found strength and deliverance through their faith.

Ekron Malcolm

By meditating on these stories and passages, believers can draw inspiration from the examples of faith and courage that abound in the Bible. Meditation on God's Word serves as a means of spiritual nourishment, rejuvenating the soul and providing sustenance for the journey of faith. It deepens the personal relationship with God, fostering a sense of closeness and trust. It becomes a powerful tool for self-examination, promoting personal growth and transformation. Through meditation, believers continuously seek to align their lives with the divine plan, striving for a more righteous and virtuous existence.

Meditating on God's Word helps individuals grow spiritually and fosters community and fellowship among believers. When Christians gather to study and meditate on the Scriptures, they share their insights, provide encouragement, and support one another. This communal experience enhances everyone's understanding of the Scriptures, strengthens their bonds, and unites them in their faith journey. This practice is not limited to any specific denomination, and it brings together Christians from diverse backgrounds seeking spiritual empowerment and growth.

The importance of meditation on God's Word, as highlighted in verses like Joshua 1:8 and Psalm 1:2, cannot be overstated. This practice enables believers to internalize God's teachings, gain guidance and wisdom, experience spiritual nourishment, and deepen their connection with Jesus Christ, our Lord and Saviour. As a result, Christians are better equipped to lead a life in accordance with God's will and experience a sense of prosperity and success in their spiritual journey. This practice is a cornerstone of a fulfilling spiritual life that benefits individuals and fosters a sense of community among believers.

Breaking the Bondage to Fear

The Essence of Christian Meditation

Christian meditation is distinct from secular or Eastern meditation practices. It involves a deliberate focus on the truths and principles found within the Bible. It is an intentional act of contemplation and reflection on the Word of God, allowing its profound wisdom to permeate our minds and hearts.

The Role of Daily Meditation

Meditation on Scripture is not a sporadic or occasional practice but a daily habit that nourishes our faith and strengthens our spiritual foundation. Just as we need daily nourishment for our physical bodies, our souls require the sustenance of God's Word through daily meditation.

Musing on God's Word

In Christian meditation, we are called to "muse" on God's Word, which means specifically and thoughtfully considering its meaning and implications. It involves reading a passage, contemplating its significance, and allowing it to resonate and bring soundness of mind and discipline of spirit within us. Meditating on Scripture opens us to divine revelation and a deeper understanding of God's character and promises. I cherish my moments of meditation. I affirm the truth of the word of God, and as I meditate on it, I cultivate inner strength. Indeed, during my meditation, the Spirit of God actively influences and empowers me, and I sense His anointing. I employ the word of God to fortify my mind, faith, and trust in Him. How do I achieve this? By embracing its truth and acknowledging it as my reality. I articulate and internalize its messages, truly believing and accepting them. I actively align myself with what the word of God declares about my identity in Christ.

The Transformative Power of Meditation

Meditation on God's Word has transformative power. It enriches our understanding of Scripture, strengthens our faith, bolsters our resilience, and equips us to confront fear confidently. Regularly immersing ourselves in the Scriptures creates a reservoir of God's wisdom and truth in us, which becomes a source of comfort and guidance in times of fear and uncertainty.

A Source of Renewed Mindsets

Through meditation, our minds are renewed. Romans 12:2 (NIV) emphasizes the importance of this renewal: "Do not conform to the pattern of this world but be transformed by the renewing of your mind." Daily meditation on God's Word aligns our thoughts with His truth, replacing fear-based thinking with faith and trust in His promises.

Christian meditation involves dedicating time daily to read, reflect, and pray over Scripture. It can also include memorizing key verses or passages that resonate with us. As we engage in this practice, we open our hearts to receive God's guidance, wisdom, and comfort, which is essential in overcoming fear.

Breaking the Bondage to Fear

Daily Meditation for Fearless Living

The art of Christian meditation invites us to immerse ourselves in the Word of God daily. It is a spiritual discipline that nourishes our faith, renews our minds, and equips us to confront and conquer fear with unwavering confidence. As you continue to explore the word of God, you will discover how this practice can be integrated into your daily life, guiding you toward a life of bold and fearless faith.

Ekron Malcolm

Scriptures for Daily Meditation

1. 2 Timothy 1:7: "For God hath not given us the spirit of fear; but of power, and of love, and of a sound mind."

2. Isaiah 41:10: "Fear thou not; for I am with thee: be not dismayed; for I am thy God: I will strengthen thee; yea, I will help thee; yea, I will uphold thee with the right hand of my righteousness."

3. Psalm 34:4: "I sought the Lord, and he heard me, and delivered me from all my fears."

4. 1 John 4:18: "There is no fear in love; but perfect love casteth out fear: because fear hath torment. He that feareth is not made perfect in love."

5. Joshua 1:9: "Have not I commanded thee? Be strong and of a good courage; be not afraid, neither be thou dismayed: for the Lord thy God is with thee whithersoever thou goest."

6. Philippians 4:6-7: "Be careful for nothing; but in every thing by prayer and supplication with thanksgiving let your requests be made known unto God. And the peace of God, which passeth all understanding, shall keep your hearts and minds through Christ Jesus."

Breaking the Bondage to Fear

7. Romans 8:15: "For ye have not received the spirit of bondage again to fear; but ye have received the Spirit of adoption, whereby we cry, Abba, Father."

8. Psalm 56:3: "What time I am afraid, I will trust in thee."

Ekron Malcolm

Prayer to Cultivate God's Power

Heavenly Father, I thank You for the power of faith that overcomes fear and for the practical strategies that equip us to stand firm in Your presence. Today, I declare my unwavering trust in You and lift my heart in prayer to overcome fear. Heavenly Father, I thank You for the power of faith that conquers fear. Just as Daniel, Shadrach, Meshach, Abednego, and David displayed unshakable faith in the face of adversity, I declare my intent to walk in the same courage and trust in You.

Lord, thank You for Your spiritual armour of faith. I put on this armour daily, knowing it protects me from the fiery darts of fear and doubt. With Your armour, I am secure and fearless.

Heavenly Father, thank You for the powerful living word You've given us. Your word is my weapon against fear, just as it was for Jesus in the wilderness. I declare that Your word is a lamp to my feet and a light to my path, guiding me away from fear and toward faith. Lord, I will meditate daily on Your word. My mind shall be renewed as I muse on Your truths, aligning with Your perfect will. I declare that my thoughts are steadfast, trusting in Your promises and overcoming fear in Jesus' name. Amen.

Breaking the Bondage to Fear

Chapter 7

Encouragement for the Journey

As we conclude our exploration of the transformative messages found in the book of Romans, it is essential to reflect on the key takeaways of the central message and offer words of encouragement for the journey ahead.

Key Takeaways

Throughout our journey, we've uncovered profound insights. We've learned about the negative effects of fear, understanding its effects and the grip it can have on our lives. We've discovered that faith, as described in Romans, is not merely a concept but a powerful and unwavering foundation for overcoming fear.

We've explored the contrast between the concept of fear and the Spirit of adoption, emphasizing that through faith, we can experience a profound sense of belonging and security. Additionally, we've witnessed how faith empowers individuals to walk in victory, renewing their minds and transforming thought patterns,

Breaking the Bondage to Fear

ultimately leading to an abundant life marked by courage and resilience.

A central message resonating from the book of Romans is clear: faith over fear. We have repeatedly seen how faith in God's promises, love, and our adoption into His family acts as a potent antidote to fear. As we trust in Him, our fears diminish, replaced by a sense of security, hope, and a renewed mind that guides us away from the bondage to fear.

As we embark on our journeys, we must remember that the path to faith over fear is not always easy. Life presents challenges and uncertainties that can test our resolve. Yet, with the insights from Romans, we can find encouragement.

With faith as our anchor, we are well-equipped to face whatever life may bring. We can cast aside fear, renew our minds, and embrace our adoption into God's family. We can walk in victory, showing resilience in the face of setbacks, and experience an abundance of God's love that transforms us from the inside out.

So, as you continue your journey of breaking the bondage to fear, may you find peace during storms, hope in times of despair, and unwavering trust in the God who loves you. With each step, may you move closer to a life marked by courage, resilience, and the profound knowledge that faith over fear is the key to a victorious and fulfilling journey.

As you close this book, I urge you to embark on your journey of faith and courage. Here are specific guidance and next steps:

1. Deepen Your Faith: Commit to a deeper relationship with God through prayer, Scripture study, and meditation.

2. Practice Courage: Face your fears with faith. Take practical steps to overcome them, knowing that God is with you.

3. Share God's Love: Extend the love you have received from God to others. Be a source of encouragement and support for those around you.

4. Should you require assistance in prayer and counselling to overcome the grip of fear that has ensnared you, remember that you are not alone. Feel free to schedule an appointment with me for spiritual counselling and deliverance.

May you walk confidently in faith, knowing that God's love, promises, and presence are always with you. May you cast aside fear and embrace the freedom of trusting in Him.

As you apply the principles from this book in your life, may you find peace amid storms, hope in times of despair, and unwavering faith in the face of fear. May your journey be marked by courage, and may your life be a testimony to the transforming power of faith. May you find many blessings upon your journey of living fearlessly in faith.

Further ahead in this book, you will find more resources to help you pursue freedom in Christ Jesus.

Breaking the Bondage to Fear

Discussion Questions for Further Reflection

For individuals or study groups seeking to dive deeper into the themes of faith and fear in the book of Romans, here are some discussion questions:

1. What role does fear play in your life, and how has it affected your faith journey?

2. How has faith helped you overcome fear in your personal experiences?

3. How can understanding God's unconditional love help you overcome specific fears or anxieties in your life?

4. Reflect on a time when you faced a fear with faith. What were the results, and what did you learn from that experience?

5. Consider the practical solutions discussed in the book. Which ones resonate with you, and how do you plan to incorporate them into your daily life?

6. Share your thoughts on the personal stories of individuals who overcame fear through faith. How do their journeys inspire you?

7. What steps will you take to cultivate and maintain godly confidence as you continue your faith journey?

These discussion questions are designed to foster reflection, meaningful conversations, and personal growth as you explore the themes of faith and fear through the lens of the book of Romans.

Breaking the Bondage to Fear

Prayers for Breaking Patterns of Habitual Sins

Breaking the Patterns of Habitual Sins:

Heavenly Father, I humbly come before You, recognizing the destructive patterns of sin. Your Word in Ezekiel 36:26 (NIV) promises, "I will give you a new heart and put a new spirit in you; I will remove from you your heart of stone and give you a heart of flesh." Lord, transform my heart, breaking the chains of sin, and create in me a heart that beats in rhythm with Your grace and righteousness. May Your Spirit empower me to resist the lure of habitual sins, and may my life be a testament to Your redeeming power in the name of Jesus. Amen.

Breaking Free from the Power of Darkness:

Lord Jesus, I stand on the truth of Romans 7:24-25 (NIV), "What a wretched man I am! Who will rescue me from this body that is subject to death? Thanks be to God, who delivers me through Jesus Christ our Lord!" In moments of weakness and darkness, I declare my dependence on Your delivering power. You are my rescuer, and in You, I find strength to break free from the power of darkness. I declare that I am not subject to the dominion of sin but am victorious through Christ in whose name I pray. Amen.

Ekron Malcolm

Accepting the Promise of God's Deliverance:

Merciful God, I take refuge in Your promise of deliverance through Jesus Christ. Your Word assures me in Romans 8:1-2 (NIV), "Therefore, there is now no condemnation for those who are in Christ Jesus because through Christ Jesus the law of the Spirit who gives life has set you free from the law of sin and death." I embrace the freedom and deliverance found in Christ. Thank You for the sacrifice of Your Son, who has redeemed me and set me free. I choose to walk in the victory You have provided in Jesus' name. Amen.

Breaking the Bondage to Fear

APPENDICES

More Helpful Resources

Breaking the Bondage to Fear

Holy Spirit Counselling Corner

What About Virtual Counselling?

Virtual or online Spiritual counselling allows individuals, couples, or families to access Spiritual support right from the comfort of their homes or any location with an internet connection.

How Online Spiritual Counseling Works:

1) Session Format: Online spiritual counselling sessions typically follow a format similar to in-person sessions. Clients discuss their concerns, feelings, and experiences with the therapist, who provides guidance, support, and therapeutic techniques to address these issues.

2) Privacy and Security: Privacy and security are essential in virtual counselling. We use secure, HIPAA-compliant platforms to protect sensitive information and maintain confidentiality.

The Effectiveness of Virtual Counselling Compared to In-Person Counselling Depends on Various Factors:

1. Accessibility: Online spiritual counselling offers greater accessibility to those seeking spiritual support, especially

those in remote areas or with limited mobility. It can also reduce barriers related to stigma, transportation, and scheduling conflicts.

2. Convenience: Virtual counselling is convenient, allowing clients to participate from the comfort of their homes and encouraging individuals to seek help who are reluctant to do so.

3. Effectiveness: Numerous studies and research articles suggest that virtual counselling can be just as effective as in-person counselling

4. Technical Issues: Technical glitches, such as poor internet connectivity or hardware problems, can occasionally disrupt virtual counselling sessions, affecting the overall experience. So, make sure you have a good internet connection.

In conclusion, virtual counselling is a valuable and effective means of accessing spiritual support. While it may not be the ideal choice for everyone, it offers accessibility, convenience, and effectiveness comparable to in-person counselling for many individuals seeking help for various biblical and spiritual issues. The choice between virtual and in-person counselling ultimately depends on individual preferences and circumstances.

Spiritual Counselling Questions

Spiritual Background:
1) What is your spiritual or religious background? (e.g., faith tradition, beliefs, practices)

Current Spiritual Struggles:
2) Can you describe the specific spiritual challenges or darkness you are currently facing?

Seeking Spiritual Guidance:
3) Have you sought spiritual guidance or support before? If yes, please provide details.

Impact on Daily Life:
4) How is the spiritual darkness impacting your daily life, relationships, and overall well-being?

Coping Mechanisms:
5) What coping mechanisms or spiritual practices have you tried to manage or overcome these challenges?

Support System:
6) Do you have a support system within your spiritual or religious community, or are you seeking support outside of it?

Medical History:
7) Are you currently taking any medications? [ ] Yes [ ] No
   If yes, please provide details:

8) Do you have any medical conditions that may be relevant to your mental health?

Mental Health History:
9) Have you received counselling or mental health treatment before? [ ] Yes [ ] No
   If yes, please provide details:

Breaking the Bondage to Fear

10) Do you have a history of psychiatric or psychological diagnoses? [ ] Yes [ ] No. If yes, please provide details:

Goals for Spiritual Counseling:
11) What are your goals or expectations for spiritual counselling?

12) How do you envision resolving or alleviating the spiritual darkness you're experiencing?

For more information

Harvest Call Ministries
293 Port Union Road,
Scarborough, ON M1C 2L3
www.freefromdarkness.com
www.harvestcall.ca

Notes

Chapter 1

Chronic Stress News Research Articles - Page 3 of 3. https://neurosciencenews.com/neuroscience-terms/chronic-stress/page/3/

Breaking the Bondage to Fear

Ekron Malcolm

About the Author

Ekron Malcolm, the author of this book, has dedicated more than 22 years to pastoral ministry, pastoral counselling, and the ministry of healing and deliverance. From a remarkably young age, at just five years old, he began his lifelong journey of faith and service, witnessing the awe-inspiring power of God firsthand.

As a seasoned pastor, Ekron has been at the forefront of guiding and shepherding congregations through the complexities of life, offering unwavering support, counsel, and spiritual guidance. His extensive experience in pastoral counselling has allowed him to touch the lives of countless individuals, providing a safe and compassionate space for healing and restoration.

Pastor Ekron has become a beacon of hope for those bound by the chains of fear. Through his ministry, he has witnessed the profound transformation of hundreds of individuals who have found freedom from the suffocating grip of fear. This remarkable journey of empowering others to break free from fear has been a cornerstone of his life's work.

Currently serving as the pastor of Harvest Call Ministries in Toronto, Canada, Pastor Ekron continues to lead his congregation passionately in the pursuit of faith, courage, and spiritual growth. His ministry is marked by a deep commitment to helping others experience God's boundless love and transformative power.

Breaking the Bondage to Fear

This book, born out of Pastor Ekron's extensive experience, deep faith, and profound understanding of the human spirit, is a testament to his dedication to spreading the message that faith is the ultimate antidote to fear. Readers can benefit from the wisdom and insights gained from years of ministry and personal experiences through these pages.

Pastor Ekron invites you to embark on a journey of faith and courage, and as you engage with the words within these pages, may you discover the transformative power of faith that overcomes fear, just as he has witnessed in the lives of so many.

Ekron Malcolm

www.ingramcontent.com/pod-product-compliance
Lightning Source LLC
Chambersburg PA
CBHW061338040426
42444CB00011B/2980